Davis Johnson

D1372920

Published by SuperSummary, www.supersummary.com

ISBN: 9798371849366

For more information or to learn about our complete library of study guides, please visit http://www.supersummary.com.

Please submit comments or questions to: http://www.supersummary.com/support/

Table of Contents

Summary

[handwritten: start reading here and write notes on note pages]

Douglas Adams's *The Hitchhiker's Guide to the Galaxy* first appeared in book form in 1979, after Adams originally conceived it as a radio play. *The Hitchhiker's Guide to the Galaxy* explores and satirizes many facets of modern life, such as the legitimacy of authority, the absurdity of bureaucracy, and the search for the ultimate answer to the question of life, the universe, and everything. *[handwritten: Themes]* The book follows the galactic exploits of Arthur Dent, the last surviving Earthman, and Ford Prefect, originally of Betelgeuse, who escape the Earth immediately before its destruction at the hands of the Vogons. They meet up with Ford's cousin and President of the Galaxy, Zaphod Beeblebrox, and his girlfriend, Trillian (also a former resident of Earth).

The Hitchhiker's Guide to the Galaxy has enjoyed a long afterlife, spawning BBC television programs, a video game, a feature film, and numerous sequels. Adams himself penned an additional four books, while a sixth book in the series, composed by the writer Eoin Colfer, was published eight years after Adams's death. Adams's work has remained a milestone in modern science-fiction writing, inspiring other writers in the genre and maintaining a widespread readership. There are two asteroids named in commemoration of Adams and his work, streets and lecture series named in his honor, and "Towel Day" is still celebrated every May 25th, more than twenty years after Adams's death.

All quotations in this guide come from the 1991 Longmeadow Press edition.

Content Warning: This guide contains some mild profanity and mentions of depression and death by suicide.

Plot Summary

Interspersed with entries from *The Hitchhiker's Guide to the Galaxy*—the fictional creation of the author of *The Hitchhiker's Guide to the Galaxy*—the book recounts the adventures of Arthur Dent, unlikely hero and last surviving Earthman, and Ford Prefect, an alien from Betelgeuse stranded on Earth for the past fifteen years. The book begins on a Thursday, as Arthur wakes up nursing a hangover. He sees yellow blurs outside his window and wonders why he drank too much at the pub the night before.

It takes him a few moments to realize that the yellow blurs are bulldozers and that they have been sent to knock down his house. It is being demolished to make way for a new bypass.

Arthur runs outside and lies down in the pathway of the bulldozers, while a local official tries to reason with him. His friend, Ford Prefect, shows up at the scene and convinces Arthur to go with him to the pub. Ford knows something that Arthur does not: He need not worry about his home because the Earth itself is about to be demolished by the Vogons. These Galactic Civil Servants have been sent to clear the way for a hyperspatial bypass.

Ford manages to rescue Arthur and himself before the Earth is destroyed, hitching a ride on the Vogon ship. However, the Vogons are infamously unpleasant, and they despise hitchhikers. Ford lends Arthur his copy of the electronic book, *The Hitchhiker's Guide to the Galaxy,* so that Arthur can understand what is going on. Unfortunately, they are discovered by the Vogons and forced to endure the captain's reading of his poetry—the "third worst in the Universe" (45). They are then escorted to the airlock, where they are thrown into "*the total vacuum of space*" (53). While they only have about thirty seconds to live, a passing spaceship—the Heart of Gold, recently stolen by the President of the Galaxy, Zaphod Beeblebrox—picks them up. Marvin, a robot with depression, escorts the men to the bridge of the ship. Ford is shocked to see his cousin, Zaphod, at the helm.

Arthur claims to have met Zaphod back on Earth—though Zaphod, at that time, did not have the extra head and arm that he now has and was called "Phil" (73). Arthur alleges that Zaphod gatecrashed an Earth party, swooped in and went off with Arthur's love interest, Trillian. Just then, Trillian walks onto the bridge. It appears as if "'this sort of thing [is] going to happen every time we use the Improbability Drive'" (74). The Infinite Improbability Drive powers the Heart of Gold, a form of miraculous transport that makes the building of hyperspatial bypasses moot. Thus, the destruction of Earth was utterly pointless.

Zaphod is on a mission to discover the legendary planet of Magrathea, once home to the designer planet industry. He is unclear about the reason for his mission; in fact, he discovers that he himself has severed certain parts of both of his brains in order to hide his motives from himself. After a narrow escape from some ancient nuclear warheads, the Heart of Gold successfully lands on Magrathea, the planet many believe was merely a myth. Zaphod, Ford, and Trillian go off to explore, while Arthur and Marvin are left to "guard" the ship. While the first three are quickly rendered unconscious by a gas released as they descend into the underground bunkers, Arthur stumbles upon an old man who takes him into the heart of Magrathea.

Slartibartfast, the old man, reveals some highly disturbing news: Earth is actually one of their designer planets, commissioned by a very intelligent species of pandimensional beings, disguised as mice. Earth was built as a kind of organic computing device, its purpose to calculate the question to life, the universe, and everything. As Arthur discovers, the answer —"forty-two" (120)—was enigmatic, so this species has their super-computer, Deep Thought, draw up the plans for an even more sophisticated computer to devise the question. This turns out to be the Earth.

Slartibartfast tells Arthur that the mice are quite excited to meet him, and they find the rest of the group to fill them in on the story of Earth. It was destroyed, unfortunately, "'five minutes before the program was completed'" (127). Thus, the mice have commissioned a new planet, Earth II, but with the discovery that Arthur was present on the planet just before its destruction, the mice determine that his brain likely holds the ultimate question. Arthur is unwilling to hand over his brain to the mice. Just as it looks as if he will have no choice, sirens blare and chaos ensues: The intergalactic police have caught up with Zaphod for stealing the Heart of Gold. He, Arthur, Ford, and Trillian escape the mice, only to be pursued by the cops who are shooting at them. Suddenly, the shooting ceases and all is quiet. It appears as if the cops' life support systems have failed. In addition, Slartibartfast leaves his aircar behind. The four can escape back to the ship. They find Marvin in a heap, full of self-loathing. He has been talking to the police officers' spacecraft, and the craft, which is responsible for the life support systems of the cops, has died by suicide.

The four humanoids and Marvin escape in the Heart of Gold, ready to embark on a whole new adventure—lunch. Zaphod directs the ship to head to the Restaurant at the End of the Universe, which will be the title of the second book in the series.

Background

Socio-Cultural Context: The Origins of a Cult Classic

Published at the end of the 1970s, *The Hitchhiker's Guide to the Galaxy* is representative of many of the preoccupations of the time. After surviving the depredations of the Second World War and the subsequent need to rebuild bombed-out buildings and ration household necessities, England experienced a renaissance of art and culture, characterized by the so-called "Swinging 60s" in London. There was also an awakening public political consciousness during this time, activated by the Cold War between the West, represented by the democracies of Western Europe and America, primarily, and the East, represented by communist-led Russia and its many satellite countries in Eastern Europe. The war in Vietnam was a particularly galvanizing event for anti-war protestors in America and Europe. However, the optimism and activism that characterized the 1960s gave way to a growing cynicism throughout the 1970s, sparked by economic uncertainty and the tense political climate. At the same time, there was also rapidly-developing technology, particularly in mass communications.

Adams's novel satirizes consumer capitalism and government bureaucracy. In the introductory section of the book, the narrator notes that people's happiness appears to be tied to "the movements of small green pieces of paper" (5)—money—which is his first direct critique of capitalism. Later, in his exploration of the history of the fictional planet, Magrathea, Adams again points out the irony of unchecked consumption and the resulting imbalance of wealth: Because Magrathea's designer planets are so wildly successful and so wildly expensive, it becomes the wealthiest civilization in the Galaxy, thus bankrupting everyone else. The only signs of life throughout the impoverished Galaxy are "the pen scratchings of scholars" writing "little treatises on the value of a planned political economy" (78), which reflects wider concerns about how to control inflation and how to ensure equality of resources during Adams's era. Adams also questions the authority of people or institutions in positions of power throughout the book, in keeping with the cultural attitudes of those who came of age in the post-war period.

His work is also influenced by the explosion of popular culture at the time, particularly film and television, such as the satirical humor of Monty Python and the launch of *Star Wars* in 1977. The absurdist humor of Monty Python's *Flying Circus* debuted on the BBC in 1969, and their later movies would also display an irreverence toward authority that is the hallmark of Adams's work as a whole. In their first film, *Monty Python and the Holy* Grail (1975), the troupe critiques capitalism in general, "imperialist dogma," authoritarian rule, and the entire class system on which England's social hierarchy is based. Adams himself would appear in two episodes of *Flying Circus*, and he worked with Graham Chapman, one of the troupe members, on other, non-Python projects.

Star Wars wielded another kind of influence, specifically the use of certain science-fiction tropes. The drinking game that Ford Prefect recalls in order to cajole Arthur into going to the pub with him, rather than protect his home from the bulldozers, is akin to a Jedi mind trick: Arthur's "will begin[s] to weaken" under the force of Ford's thoughts (13). Later, when Zaphod describes his youthful exploits with Yooden Vranx, it echoes Han Solo's bragging about the speed of the Millennium Falcon: "We get in his trijet [. . .] crossed three parsecs in a matter of weeks, [and] bust our way into a megafreighter I still don't know how" (125). There is even a passing reference to *A Clockwork Orange*: When Arthur and Ford are subjected to the painful recitation of Vogon poetry, they are strapped to chairs and forced to listen (45), just as Alex is forced to watch the ultra-violent images that will condition him against violence in Stanley Kubrick's 1971 film.

There were also scientific discoveries and technological developments gaining cultural traction at the time, which clearly influenced Adams's work. From the emerging understanding of quantum physics to the fledgling field of chaos theory, Adams employs humorous explanations and conundrums that reflect these scientific breakthroughs. For example, in creating the Infinite Improbability Drive, Adams satirizes the randomness of astrophysics and quantum physics. The "Brownian Motion producer" that powers finite machines is actually "a nice hot cup of tea" and can be utilized as a party trick: "such generators were often used to break the ice at parties by making all the molecules in a hostess's undergarments leap simultaneously one foot to the left, in accordance with the Theory of Indeterminacy" (60). Adams's preoccupation with improbability and coincidence engages with concepts derived from chaos theory, that all actions have reverberations across space and time. Arthur's careless words falling through a wormhole and initiating a thousand-year-war in a faraway galaxy are just one example (129).

Adams also seems to anticipate the development of technologies: Computers and androids with human personalities and independent intellectual capacities anticipate Artificial Intelligence; *The Hitchhiker's Guide to the Galaxy*, as represented within the text, is "a sort of electronic book" (37), an e-book ahead of its time; and the notion that people's lives "are governed by telephone numbers" (70) presages the singular significance of the cell phone. Finally, Adams's suggestion that the Earth is really a kind of "organic computer" (110)—a computer designed to calculate the question to the answer of life, the universe, and everything—sounds remarkably similar to recent ideas proposed by the Simulation Hypothesis. This Hypothesis suggests that the world in which humanity thinks it exists is, in fact, a computer simulation. It seems certain that Adams would be delighted by such a possibility.

Chapter Summaries & Analyses

Introduction and Chapters 1-7

Introduction Summary

The author describes Earth as "an utterly insignificant little blue-green planet whose ape-descended life forms are so amazingly primitive that they still think digital watches are a pretty neat idea" (5). The author continues to say that the book that will follow is "the story of [a] terrible, stupid catastrophe and some of its consequences," as well as the story of a "wholly remarkable book," *The Hitchhiker's Guide to the Galaxy* (5).

Chapter 1 Summary

The book begins as Arthur Dent wakes up, nursing a hangover and wondering why he overindulged at the pub the night before. He feels troubled by something but cannot quite remember what the problem is. He notices a couple of yellow bulldozers outside the window of his ordinary house on the outskirts of an ordinary village in England. When he finally makes the connection—the bulldozers have come to raze his house in order to construct a bypass—he runs out into the yard and sprawls in the mud in front of the bulldozers, trying to save his home.

Mr. L. Prosser, an emissary from the local council, reminds Arthur that he should have known about the plans all along and made the necessary preparations. Arthur retorts that the plans were only available "in the bottom of a locked filing cabinet" in the bathroom of an unlit basement of the local planning office (10). Prosser is unimpressed, insisting that the bypass needs to be built but without specifying any reason for it.

Arthur's friend, Ford Prefect, shows up and wants to take Arthur to the pub. Ford, unbeknownst to Arthur, is not actually an Earthling: He is from Betelgeuse and has been stranded on Earth for the past fifteen years, posing as an out-of-work actor. Prefect convinces Mr. L. Prosser to stand in for Arthur and put himself in the mud in front of the bulldozers, so that Prefect can take Arthur to the pub for some drinks and a talk. While Arthur is not convinced that he can trust Prosser, he gives in to Ford's persuasion, who suggests that they can "'trust him [Prosser] to the end of the Earth'" which, disconcertingly to Arthur, is "'[a]bout twelve minutes away'" according to Ford (16).

Chapter 2 Summary

The chapter begins by comparing the *Encyclopedia Galactica's* entry on alcohol, "a colorless volatile liquid formed by the fermentation of sugars" (17), with the entry from *The Hitchhiker's Guide to the Galaxy.* Its entry waxes poetic on the intoxicating—even literally mind-blowing—impact of the Pan Galactic Gargle Blaster, which, when consumed, feels "like having your brains smashed out with a slice of lemon wrapped round a large gold brick" (17). Needless to say, the unnamed narrator tells the reader, *Hitchhiker's* sells considerably more copies than the *Encyclopedia.*

Ford orders six pints, and Arthur questions the reasonableness of drinking so much at lunchtime. Ford orders him to drink quickly, telling him that the world is going to end. Arthur complains that it must be Thursday.

Chapter 3 Summary

High above in the ionosphere, several enormous yellow spaceships are hovering, while most people on Earth are blissfully unaware. Ford Prefect, however, has picked up the ships' signal with his "Sub-Etha Sens-O-Matic"; this, along with several more extraterrestrial items—including *The Hitchhiker's Guide to the Galaxy*, for whom Prefect is a reporter—are tucked away in Prefect's carryall. At the bottom is one of Ford's most prized possessions, "a largish bath towel from Marks and Spencer" (21). As *The Hitchhiker's Guide to the Galaxy* notes, the towel "*has great practical value*"; it goes on to espouse its many uses, including "*wet[ting] it for hand-to-hand combat*," using it as a distress beacon, or drying off (21).

Ford is disappointed that Arthur does not have a towel with him, while Arthur remains skeptical of Ford's claims that the world is about to end. They hear some loud noises outside the bar, and Ford assures Arthur that this is not yet the end of the world, only his house being knocked down. Arthur runs out of the pub in distress, as Ford tips the barkeep handsomely. The barkeep, tuned in to Ford Prefect's "subliminal signal" of distress, begins to believe his extraordinary declaration about the end of the world (22-23). The bartender immediately calls for "'[l]ast orders, please'" (23).

Ford rushes to Arthur, trying to pull him away from the wreckage of the house and get him to notice the "huge yellow somethings" hovering ominously in the sky (24). Ford is dismayed to learn that the intergalactic signal he picked up the night before came from the Vogons. He is comforted only by the fact that he has his towel.

Finally, the Vogon ships try to communicate with the Earth, claiming that due to "the building of a hyperspatial express route through your star system [. . .] your planet is one of those scheduled for demolition'" (25-26). The voice of Prostenic Vogon Jeltz goes on to scold the Earthlings for their ensuing panic claiming that "'All the planning charts and demolition orders have been on display in your local planning department [. . .] for fifty of your Earth years'" (26). The Vogons proceed with the demolition.

Chapter 4 Summary

Meanwhile, Zaphod Beeblebrox, President of the Imperial Galactic Government, is traveling across the waters of Damogran to christen the newly-built—and amazingly outfitted—ship, the Heart of Gold. Beeblebrox adores the attention of the media and public. He makes his entrance in high style, floating onto the stage sitting on a sofa encased in a bubble. With his two heads and three arms, Beeblebrox is not only handsome in a roguish way but also unforgettably unusual. His casual girlfriend, Trillian, is the only one in the waiting crowd who is unimpressed by his theatrics—she has grown tired of these exploits long ago.

When Beeblebrox takes the stage, he makes a stunning announcement. He approaches the Heart of Gold, expressing his admiration for its splendor: "'That [ship] is so amazingly amazing I think I'd like to steal it'" (32). He launches a "Parolyso-Matic bomb" and takes the ship, Trillian in tow (32).

Chapter 5 Summary

The narrative returns to the Vogon ship, where the narrator explains that the Vogons are a highly unevolved species, who obliterated most of the resources on their home planet before becoming bureaucratic emissaries of the Galactic Civil Service. The narrator also relays the rather important point that the Vogons, and in particular Prostenic Vogon Jeltz, despise hitchhikers.

Arthur and Ford, meanwhile, are in the bowels of the ship, picked up by the Dentrassis, who cook for the Vogons and love to annoy them. Both are surprised by the poor condition of the ship once the lights are on, though Ford explains that "'this is a working ship'" (37). Ford hands Arthur *The Hitchhiker's Guide to the Galaxy*, an electronic book, so that Arthur can learn a little about the Vogons. The entry ends with an ominous warning: "'On no account allow a Vogon to read poetry to you'" (38).

Ford explains to Arthur that they have been rescued just in time, as Arthur's Earth has been demolished. Ford seems unaware that Arthur might be upset by this fact and cautions him not to panic—the advice extolled on the electronic book's cover. Suddenly, the loudspeakers come to life, and Arthur hears rough howling noises emerge. Ford shoves a small yellow fish in his ear, and Arthur begins to decipher the Vogon message being relayed.

Chapter 6 Summary

The Vogon captain is telling his hitchhiking passengers that they will be quickly caught and brought to him. He will first read them some of his poetry before putting them out of the airlock. Ford, in the interim, has Arthur read about the Babel fish—the amazing little creature that he has stuck in Arthur's ear, allowing him to understand the Vogon language.

Arthur's mind drifts back to what has happened. He is still in shock over Earth's destruction and moved by the loss of certain things, including Humphrey Bogart movies and McDonald's. He asks Ford for the *Guide* again, wanting to see the entry for Earth. It is surprisingly brief: "'Harmless'" (44). Arthur is upset by the brevity and dismissive tone of the entry. Ford shrugs and says that, after his fifteen years of research, he has recommended the entry be updated to "'Mostly harmless.'" They hear footsteps echoing through the hallway. The Vogons have found them.

Chapter 7 Summary

Prostetnic Vogon Jeltz insists on reading his poetry—widely known as "the third worst in the Universe" (45)—to his interlopers. They are "strapped in" to "Poetry Appreciation chairs" (45) for their enjoyment. The poetry is excruciating for both Arthur and Ford, who scream and groan in pain. However, when the Vogon asks them to compliment his poetry, Arthur surprises Ford by saying, "'Actually I quite liked it'" (46). Ford realizes that if they flatter the Vogon enough, perhaps they will avoid being forcibly ejected from the airlock. Their plan fails.

They are taken to their fate by a junior guard, who appears to enjoy shouting at them. Ford tries to gain his sympathy by suggesting that the drudgery of his job divorces him from the more gratifying experiences— like culture and art—the world has to offer. While the guard thinks about this for a moment, he decides that job security is more appealing and that he likes shouting at people. He shoves Arthur and Ford into the outer airlock. Arthur laments that all that will be left of Earth are the words "mostly harmless" from *The Hitchhiker's Guide*. The hatch opens, and the men are ejected into outer space.

Chapters 1-7 Analysis

In the introduction, Adams previews what the book will be about as well as introducing his absurdist humor, which nearly always conceals an underlying philosophical point. The fact that the inhabitants of Earth— itself located in "the uncharted backwaters of the unfashionable end of the Western Spiral arm of the Galaxy" (5)—are largely unhappy, reveals the author's satirical bent: The insignificance of this "backwater" lolling about in its "unfashionable" region serves to foreshadow not only the insignificance of the planet but also the triviality of said human unhappiness in the face of annihilation. The narrator notes that most of the solutions to this unhappiness are connected to money, "which is odd because on the whole it wasn't the small green pieces of paper that were unhappy" (5), thereby critiquing capitalist consumption and the existential emptiness it leaves behind. He also hints, as the Earth is casually destroyed to make way for a bypass, that life is inherently pointless.

In the grand scheme of things, the relative happiness of a minor species within the larger galaxy might be inconsequential, but Adams's characters certainly do not see it that way. Arthur Dent feels concern about the destruction of his personal residence, while also grasping its unimportance given that the entire Earth is about to be destroyed. Adams creates a clash between the quotidian—the looming destruction of Arthur Dent's unremarkable house—and the galactic, the complete annihilation of the Earth, to put things firmly in perspective. While Arthur's world extends only to the microcosm of a small house "which more or less exactly failed to please the eye" (7), Ford Prefect's world extends to the macrocosm of the entire universe. Nevertheless, this universe looks an awful lot like the one Arthur is forced to leave behind. The yellow bulldozers that threaten to destroy Arthur's home are mirrored in the "huge yellow somethings [. . .] screaming through the sky" (24) which turn out to be the ships of the Vogons, emissaries of the Galactic Civil Service, who have come to vaporize the Earth because it is in the pathway of a planned intergalactic expressway. Thus, the Earth itself becomes as insignificant as Arthur's personal property: Nothing is sacred under the control of faceless bureaucracy.

Bureaucracy is an important thematic element in the novel on both a small and large scale, with special satirical emphasis placed on its absurdity and inefficiency. When Arthur hears that the plans for his house's destruction have long been in the local planning office, Arthur points out that they were "in the bottom of a locked filing cabinet stuck in a disused lavatory with a sign on the door saying 'Beware of the Leopard'" (10), emphasizing the inaccessibility and obscure nature of bureaucracy's inner workings. A similar situation occurs with the Galactic Civil Service and their Vogon emissaries. When the Vogons inform the Earthlings that the plans for the hyperspatial highway have been available for fifty years in Alpha Centauri, the Vogons insist that it does not matter that Alpha Centauri is unreachable via Earth's technology, insisting that it is the Earthlings' fault "if [they] can't be bothered to take an interest in local affairs" (26). The bureaucratic forces that rule deliberately keep the locals uninformed so that the machinery of industry and so-called progress can rumble ever forward.

The Hitchhiker's Guide to the Galaxy also contains a meta-fictive version of itself, Ford Prefect's electronic copy of *The Hitchhiker's Guide to the Galaxy*. This e-book provides information that emphasizes the absurdity of the universe—describing items such as the Pan Galactic Gargle Blaster and allowing the author to devolve into wild tangents—while also revealing the anti-authoritarian streak in the novel. In its first extended mention, *The Guide* is compared to the rather staid *Encyclopedia Galactica*, whose definition of alcohol is just that—a dry, direct definition. *The Guide*, on the other hand, details the delights of the Pan Galactic Gargle Blaster, even going so far as to provide a (ridiculously complicated) recipe. The institutional version of the truth, as represented by the *Encyclopedia*, is undermined by the irreverent tone of *The Guide*. In this way, *The Guide* within *The Hitchhiker's Guide to the Galaxy* reflects one of the novel's key themes, **The Absurdity of Modern Bureaucracy**.

Adams also critiques authority in the form of leadership. In describing Zaphod Beeblebrox's role as President of the Imperial Galactic Government, the narrator remarks, "Only six people in the Galaxy knew that the job of the Galactic President was not to wield power but to attract attention away from it" (29). The narrator also adds, "Zaphod Beeblebrox was amazingly good at his job" (29). This critique suggests that real power operates behind the scenes, out of the public eye, while the populace remains in thrall to the antics of charismatic leaders. Thus, the shadowy web of true power can operate unseen, unchallenged, and immune to the will of the people, with democracy merely a fiction to assuage the uninformed masses. Ironically, however, although Beeblebrox's theft of the Heart of Gold might at first appear to be a mere publicity stunt, it turns out to attract the attention of those in *actual* power.

Finally, Arthur and Ford face an uncertain fate by the end of these chapters. Arthur muses on what he feels as the last surviving Earthling. Once more, a wider tragedy is embodied and experienced in the form of a smaller one: Instead of reacting emotionally to the loss of the entire earth, Arthur experiences direct emotion only when recalling the loss of his own homeland: "England no longer existed. He'd got that—somehow he'd got it," while the loss of America is something "He couldn't grasp" (43). Furthermore, in reflecting upon the loss of "Bogart movies" and "McDonald's" (43)—some of the cultural capitalist hallmarks of the "American century"—Arthur alludes to the consumerism of the era, reflecting once more the domination of widespread capitalist ventures such as Hollywood and fast food and the homogenization of the modern era.

Chapters 8-14

Chapter 8 Summary

Arthur and Ford have been ejected into space. The narrator interjects an entry from *The Hitchhiker's Guide to the Galaxy*: "Space is big. Really big. You just won't believe how vastly hugely mind-bogglingly big it is'" (53). To this end, the book suggests, the odds of Arthur and Ford getting picked up by a passing ship in the vastness of space are truly astronomical. Further, the numerical odds happen to correspond to a telephone number on Earth where Arthur once met a lovely girl. Then, astoundingly, Arthur and Ford "were rescued" (54).

Chapter 9 Summary

Arthur and Ford's rescue coincides with a hole opening up in the universe. Several improbable events happen at once: besides Arthur and Ford's rescue, celebratory balloons and hats were dropped on the universe; more than two hundred thousand fried eggs were dropped on a starving tribe in a different galaxy; and the pair are gripped by "vicious storms of unreason" (55). They experience a series of unsettling transformations, with Arthur watching his arm drift away while Ford slowly turns into a penguin. Eventually, a soothing voice comes across the intercom: "'Welcome,' the voice said, 'to the Starship Heart of Gold'" (58). The voice assures the men that normalcy will soon be restored—but not before a horde of monkeys wants them to review their script of *Hamlet*.

Chapter 10 Summary

The Infinite Improbability Drive "is a wonderful new method of crossing vast interstellar distances in a mere nothingth of a second, without all that tedious mucking about in hyperspace" (60). Physicists thought this kind of invention "was virtually impossible," which inspired a student to rethink the problem. *Virtually* impossible implies that the making of the machine harbors a "*finite* improbability" of success (60). After engineering a generator, the student feeds it a hot cup of tea, and it works. After garnering awards for his invention, the student is attacked by a horde of actual physicists.

Chapter 11 Summary

Zaphod Beeblebrox and Trillian are manning the controls of the Heart of Gold, as the probability numbers continue to fall toward normal ranges. Beeblebrox is upset that the hitchhikers have been picked up, since he is running from the intergalactic law for stealing the ship. Trillian informs him that she did not pick up the strays—the ship itself did, on its own.

Beeblebrox orders the onboard android, Marvin, to retrieve the two men. Marvin is "'feeling very depressed'" as he feels that life is pointless (63). *The Guide* explains that the Sirius Cybernetics Corporation had the idea of infusing their robots with particular personalities, much to the chagrin of people having to work with them. Marvin, reluctantly, goes to retrieve Arthur and Ford, complaining about life. He tells the pair that the ship has been stolen by Zaphod Beeblebrox, who would like to see them. Ford responds with astonishment.

Chapter 12 Summary

Meanwhile, Zaphod is listening to the "sub-etha radio bands" for news of himself (67). Trillian thinks something is suspect about this coincidence: she herself was picked up by Zaphod in this very same sector of space. When she crunches the numbers, the improbability of this happenstance is "an irrational number that only has a conventional meaning in Improbability Physics" (69). That is, it is so improbable as to be nearly impossible.

Chapter 13 Summary

Arthur and Ford are led to the bridge of the ship by Marvin. When they encounter Zaphod Beeblebrox, something odd occurs: Arthur believes he has met the man before at a party in Islington. Back then, he was "Phil," and he left the party with a woman Arthur was interested in. Arthur seethes with fury at Zaphod's callous coolness, while Ford gapes in disbelief: not only does Arthur know his cousin, Zaphod Beeblebrox, but also he realizes that Beeblebrox left him stranded on Earth. Trillian comes into sight of Arthur; she is the young woman who left the party with Beeblebrox. Arthur exclaims, "'Tricia McMillan? [. . .] What are you doing here?'" (74). The improbability stakes continue to rise.

Chapter 14 Summary

The group ponders why they have been brought together. Trillian cannot sleep because she is upset upon learning of the destruction of Earth. She, Arthur, and two white mice are all that is left of the planet. Zaphod cannot sleep because he is bothered by the improbability of his own actions, much less what brought Arthur and Ford into his orbit. Ford cannot sleep because he is excited to be back in the universe with his cousin. Arthur sleeps soundly, exhausted by his exploits.

In the morning, Trillian informs Zaphod that she thinks they have found what he has been looking for.

Chapters 8-14 Analysis

The narrator echoes the introduction to the book, which emphasizes the vastness of space and thus the unlikely rescue of Arthur and Ford in the thirty seconds they have to survive outside of the Vogon ship's airlock. This improbable occurrence sets the tone for the next few chapters. The author conflates coincidence with destiny, physics with fate, and then parodies his own comparisons. On the one hand, the narrative suggests that the universe is a place of unfathomable harmony, where everything happens for a reason—the characters are brought together for some ultimate, yet-to-be-determined, conclusion. On the other hand, the narrative mockingly questions the very idea of fate, with randomness ruling the day.

It is not only the improbability of the rescue that opens the door for this mockery but also the attitude, personified by the android Marvin, about the pointless nature of existence. With the invention of an Infinite Improbability Drive, the author satirizes the emerging field of quantum physics and its upending of traditional scientific consensus about how the universe works. For instance, the Infinite Improbability Drive is sparked into life by "a fresh cup of really hot tea" (60)—like an Englishman waking up in the morning. The Frankenstein-like creation allows the ridiculousness to proliferate: Arthur watches his limbs detach, as Ford transmogrifies into a penguin. The author also employs the very symbol of randomness, "The Infinite Monkey Theorem," which posits that an infinite number of monkeys typing on an infinite number of keyboards will eventually produce *Hamlet*, one of Shakespeare's greatest plays. The problem is that the very definition of infinity prevents the theorem from ever being proved via the traditional scientific method, wherein measuring and testing cannot occur—infinity exists only as a concept, not as a physical reality.

The improbability number that represents the odds of Arthur and Ford's rescue happens to be "the telephone number of an Islington flat where Arthur once went to a very good party and met a very nice girl" (54) who turns out to be Trillian. She reacts to the numbers with a gasp as well. The implication is that the probability of the pair's rescue is, absurdly and coincidentally, Trillian's old phone number on Earth. The narration therefore keeps alive the tensions between a determinist view and random view of the universe, leaving how much is truly random as an open-ended question.

Marvin, the robot with depression, embodies the view that existence is pointless, with his fatalistic attitude and rejection of all happiness. Not only do the cheery whirring sounds of the doors drive him to distraction, he also openly displays "his utter contempt and horror of all things human" (63). Marvin's exaggerated world-weariness satirizes existentialist navel-gazing in the modern era, while also directly invoking comparisons to the famously indecisive Hamlet, who cannot act in the face of difficult choices. Marvin does not act, believing that it does not matter, since everyone is doomed in the end.

The narrator again ridicules various kinds of authority throughout these chapters, such as the angry mob of respectable physicists attacking the student responsible for the Infinite Improbability Drive. Representative officials and authorized institutions are depicted ironically. Even the very laws of physics come under question in this unlikely quest. The final chapter here returns to the problem of improbability, as Beeblebrox announces that they have just found "'the most improbable planet that ever existed'" (77). In Adams's hands, improbability becomes the most probable of plot developments.

Chapters 15-21

Chapter 15 Summary

This short chapter consists of an entry from *The Hitchhiker's Guide to the Galaxy*, describing the planet of Magrathea. Magrathea specialized in creating designer planets for the wealthiest members of the galaxy during the golden age of the Empire. The venture was so successful that

Magrathea became so absurdly wealthy that it plunged the rest of the Empire into "abject poverty" (78). Thus, they no longer had clients for whom to design planets and faded into "the obscurity of legend" (78). Nobody, it seems, believes anymore that such a planet ever existed.

Chapter 16 Summary

Arthur walks onto the bridge as Zaphod and Ford are arguing over the existence of Magrathea: Ford insists that the planet is only "'a fairy story [that] parents tell their kids about at night if they want them to grow up to be economists'" (79). All four gaze down at the planet and can at least agree that it looks very beautiful and very old. Arthur realizes something is missing: tea. Eventually, the narrator confirms that the planet below them is Magrathea. The narrator also adds that in the ensuing events, nobody will be killed, though someone will sustain a bruise to the arm— this information is relayed in advance so that the readers should not experience stress over the uncertainty of the characters' fates.

Chapter 17 Summary

Arthur goes in search of tea, which is dispensed by a Nutri-Matic machine and is "almost, but not quite, entirely unlike tea" (83). The tea revives Arthur and he joins the conversation regarding the foray onto the planet. He wonders if it is safe and Zaphod assures him that it is since it is a ghost planet. Immediately after his assurance, they are startled to hear a voice transmitted to the ship, asking them to leave. The voice begins politely, but as the ship continues to move closer to the planet, it becomes threatening, mentioning "guided missiles" that are "currently converging with [the] ship" (84). Apparently, Magrathea does not want visitors.

Zaphod tries to take control of the ship in order to attempt evasive maneuvers, but he does not really know how to fly it. He steers the ship directly into the path of the approaching missiles. It again appears as if the group are headed for certain death. They are hurled against the far wall of the cabin, unable to reach the controls. Suddenly, Arthur asks what would happen if they turned on the Infinite Improbability Drive. He can reach it, so he does: "The next thing that happened was a mind-mangling explosion of noise and light" (88).

Chapter 18 Summary

The crew are saved: "And the next thing that happened after that was that the Heart of Gold continued on its way perfectly normally with a rather fetchingly redesigned interior" (89). The ship now looks like a classical conservatory, with marble statues and a spiral staircase and a garden around the control panel. Not only has the interior of the ship been altered by the Infinite Improbability Drive, but also the missiles have been transformed into a "'a bowl of petunias and a very surprised-looking whale,'" as Ford reports (89). They are no longer in danger.

The chapter then recounts the thoughts of the whale as it plummets through the atmosphere towards the planet's surface. It questions the purpose of existence; tries to name various body parts and sensations; and wonders whether the hard surface fast coming toward it will be its friend. Then, "after a sudden wet thud, there was silence" (91). In contrast, the bowl of petunias only groans, "Oh no, not again" (91).

Chapter 19 Summary

The Heart of Gold has landed, and the four humanoids and the android prepare to disembark. Trillian cries out that her mice have escaped. The narrator points out that this seemingly trivial result of a most dramatic escape from certain death would have been taken more seriously had the crew known more of the intellectual hierarchy of Earth. The computer —whose personality has been altered by Zaphod to be more anxious instead of cheerful—reluctantly lets the crew out. A few moments later, unbeknownst to Zaphod and the rest, the computer opens the hatch again, "in response to a command that caught him entirely by surprise" (93).

Chapter 20 Summary

The surface of Magrathea is "dullish brown" and "dullish gray," devoid of any natural or manufactured feature of interest. The group soon realize that they are walking about in the muck of splattered whalemeat. However, the whale's crashlanding on the surface has opened up a fissure in the surface that leads to underground tunnels—the Magratheans were rumored to have lived underneath the unpleasant surface of their planet. Zaphod appoints Arthur and Marvin as guards to the opening, as he, Ford, and Trillian descend into the tunnels.

Ford questions Zaphod on the purpose of their visit. Zaphod responds that he really does not know, that he often wonders why he does the things that he does, from running for President of the Galaxy to stealing the Heart of Gold to searching for Magrathea. He confesses to Ford and Trillian that he went looking for some answers to his own vague motivations and underwent some brain scans. After some superimposing of results, Zaphod discovered "'A whole section in the middle of both brains that related only to each other and not to anything else around them'" because "'Some bastard had cauterized all the synapses and electronically traumatized those two lumps of cerebellum'" (98). Ford asks him if he knew who might do such a horrifying thing. Zaphod says yes, since the culprit "'left their initials burned into the cauterized synapses'" (98): Those initials are Z.B.

Zaphod Beeblebrox is about to explain more when gas starts to fill their lungs. Zaphod, Ford, and Trillian quickly pass out.

Chapter 21 Summary

Meanwhile, Arthur reads random passages from *The Hitchhiker's Guide to the Galaxy*. In one, he learns of a young man, Veet Voojagig, who determines to discover a planet where the dominant lifeform is ballpoint pens, believing this would explain where all of his lost pens ended up. Eventually, he claims that he did find such a planet, but when an expedition is sent to confirm his discovery, all that is found is a "small asteroid" (99). Still, Voojagig becomes a rich man, mysteriously paid many thousands each year, as a friend, Zaphod Beeblebrox, started a "highly profitable secondhand ballpoint business" (100).

Arthur grows tired of the book and tries to engage Marvin in conversation. The robot rebuffs every attempt, so Arthur decides to go on a walk. He stumbles across an old man.

Chapters 15-21 Analysis

In introducing readers to the legendary planet of Magrathea, Adams is able to engage in an extended critique of empire and the inevitable inequitable distribution of wealth and resources that follows. As *The Guide* recounts the age of empire: "Many men became extremely rich, but this was perfectly natural and nothing to be ashamed of because no one was really poor—at least no one worth speaking of" (78). The passage critiques imperialism and economic inequality, as those who wield imperial power are wealthy, while those under the control of imperial power are not only poor but also not fully human ("no one worth speaking of"). The book takes this economic imbalance to its logical, if absurd, extreme. As Magrathea continues to amass wealth, the Galaxy supporting its massive fortune becomes ever poorer, which renders Magrathea's "custom-made luxury planet" services obsolete: "And so the system broke down, the Empire collapsed, and a long sullen silence settled over a billion hungry worlds" (78). The Empire's unchecked greed destroys itself from within.

The author continues his satire of consumer capitalism in the depiction of Magrathea's now-defunct services. Before the disembodied voice from the planet threatens the Heart of Gold, it assures the crew that "as soon as our business is resumed announcements will be made in all fashionable magazines and color supplements" (84). Commercial advertisements will reassure anxious potential consumers that their capitalist impulses and disposable wealth will once again be consequential—especially in distracting them from the more pressing problems of justifying their existence or contemplating inequality. These are constant preoccupations in the novel: how capitalism (and authority in general) intersect with individual needs and metaphysical instincts, raising the question of what the purpose of existence should be. In an aside, *The Guide* reveals contemptuous views of the kind of conspicuous consumption displayed by the ultra-rich: "an Antarean parakeet gland stuck on a small stick is a revolting but much-sought-after cocktail delicacy and very large sums of money are often paid for them by very rich idiots who want to impress other very rich idiots" (86-87). Amassing wealth, like justifying existence, is often portrayed as a pointless endeavor.

The author also continues to break down the traditional barriers between authority—this time, literal authorship—and the masses of potential readers. In another meta-fictive move, Adams breaks the so-called "fourth wall" that exists between the author and the reader. When Arthur and his cohorts are under threat from the Magrathean missiles, the narrator reaches out directly to the reader: "Stress and nervous tension are now serious social problems in all parts of the Galaxy [. . .] [I]n order that this situation should not be in any way exacerbated [. . .] the following facts will now be revealed in advance" (82). The narrator then goes on to assure the reader that the ship will not be destroyed and all the characters will be safe—other than the slight bruise someone will suffer. A few pages later, the narrator again breaks in to remind the reader that "the deadly nuclear missiles do not eventually hit the ship. The safety of the crew is absolutely assured" (87). The relationship between author and reader, in this scenario, is one of equals—each knows as much as the other.

Later, however, the narrator also foreshadows events and plot points. When Trillian exclaims that her mice have escaped in the chaos of dodging the missiles, the narrator steps in and draws the reader's attention to the event, revealing, "human beings were only the third most intelligent life form present on the planet Earth" (92). While giving nothing specific away, the narrator manipulates the reader's focus and withholds particular details. In this way, the meta-fictive move undercuts the egalitarian distribution of knowledge for the sake of suspense, while still flagging the disappearance of the mice as something worthy of notice.

The crew of the Heart of Gold survive another improbable escape from death via the Infinite Improbability Drive, with Arthur emerging as the equally-improbable hero. When Arthur engages the Drive, causing the missiles to transmogrify into a whale and a bowl of petunias, Zaphod exclaims, "'Hey, kid, you just saved our lives, you know that?'" (90). When Arthur humbly demurs—"'it was nothing really'"—Zaphod agrees with him: "'Oh well, forget it then'" (90). Although Arthur's heroism is immediately undermined, he remains central to the story. He is the one to summarize the underwhelming experience of reaching Magrathea, calling it "an event that should quite naturally fill one with awe" before adding, "'Pity it's such a dump though'" (94). It is also Arthur who unwittingly stumbles across the lone figure on the planet's surface who will eventually reveal its—and many others'—secrets.

Chapters 22-28

Chapter 22 Summary

The old man assures Arthur that he and his friends will not be harmed, explaining that the missiles were launched via an ancient automated system. He also explains that the inhabitants of Magrathea are not dead, as is commonly assumed, but rather that they have been sleeping, waiting for the economic environment of the Galaxy to rebound. The old man demands that Arthur come with him, "'deep into the bowels of the planet'" (103). They decide to leave Marvin behind. Finally, the old man reveals that his name is Slartibartfast, to which Arthur responds incredulously.

Chapter 23 Summary

The narrator breaks in again to explain that, while "man had always assumed that he was more intelligent than dolphins," the opposite turns out to be true (105). In fact, the dolphins had tried to warn the humans of the upcoming destruction of the Earth, but the humans had mistaken their antics for adorable play. Thus, the dolphins "left the Earth by their own means," escaping the annihilation of the planet (105). The narrator then says that there is actually another species even more intelligent than the dolphins.

Chapter 24 Summary

Slartibartfast leads Arthur down into the depths of Magrathea via an enormously speedy aircar. He reveals that he knows Arthur is an Earthling, but he does not tell him how he knows this. As they emerge onto the "'factory floor'" of Magrathea's once thriving planet-building business, Arthur is overwhelmed by the scale of the operation (108). Arthur is taken aback by one planet in particular: He sees what looks like another Earth under construction. He is even more astonished by Slartibartfast's response: "'We're making a copy from our original blueprints'" (108). He goes on to reveal that Earth was actually a designer planet, commissioned by mice—who are actually a highly-evolved, pandimensional species—built for a particular purpose. Unfortunately, it was destroyed about five minutes before said purpose was completed. Thus, the Magratheans are rebuilding the planet. Earth, in Slartibartfast's explanation, is "'an organic computer running a ten-million-year research program'" (110). Arthur has a difficult time processing this information.

Chapter 25 Summary

Slartibartfast recounts the long story of how the commission of "Earth" came to be. Millions of years in the past, there was a species intensely concerned with the great metaphysical questions of existence, such as the true purpose of life. They decided to build a great computer, "the size of a small city" (111), to answer these great questions. Deep Thought, as the computer was called, is tasked with finding the answer to the question of life, the universe, and everything. There is great controversy over this undertaking, as the influential philosophers on the planet protest that they will be out of a job if the computer comes up with the answer. However, Deep Thought informs the people that it will take at least seven and a half million years to determine the answer, during which time the philosophers can amass much fame and wealth publicizing their various theories on what that answer will be. Thus, the computer is left to do its work.

Chapter 26 Summary

Arthur interrupts Slartibartfast's story. He wonders what all of this has to do with the Earth that he knew, not to mention the pandimensional mice. Slartibartfast patiently explains that this is only the first half of the story and offers to take Arthur on a tour of the new Earth-in-progress. Arthur sadly refuses. "'[I]t wouldn't be quite the same,'" he says (116).

Chapter 27 Summary

Slartibartfast takes Arthur to his office, which is cluttered with books and maps. He offers Arthur a headset to wear, wherein Arthur will be able to witness the second half of the story as a recording. The day that Deep Thought will pronounce its answer to the ultimate question of life, the universe, and everything has finally arrived. After much fanfare and anticipation, Deep Thought slowly awakens and finally gives his answer: "'Forty-two,' said Deep Thought, with infinite majesty and calm" (120).

Chapter 28 Summary

The answer provokes an immediate uproar, to which Deep Thought patiently explains, "'I think the problem, to be quite honest with you, is that you've never actually known what the question is'" (121). This creates more turmoil until the people decide to ask Deep Thought to now calculate the question. When the great computer says that it does not have the capacity to do so, it suggests that it can build another, greater computer which can. Deep Thought names this new, ultra-computer "'the Earth'" (122).

Chapters 22-28 Analysis

Adams again critiques the capitalist system and the response of the rich to the economic collapse that they themselves engendered. As Slartibartfast admits to Arthur, the Magratheans decided to avoid the chaos of the collapse of the Galactic Empire and sleep until "'everybody else had rebuilt the economy enough to afford rather expensive services'" (102). Arthur is rather shocked by this callous admission, though Slartibartfast deflects his reaction by claiming himself to be "'a bit out of touch'" (102). The rapacious capitalists will both destroy the system that feeds them and rely on those left behind, impoverished and hungry, to clean up their economic mess. Indeed, like Slartibartfast, they are out of touch with the common people. The narration also notes that Arthur is "a regular *Guardian* reader," which serves to explain his appalled reaction (102). *The Guardian*, an English newspaper founded in the nineteenth century, is considered the paper of choice for the more liberal political left in England. Arthur's reading habits characterize (or caricature) Arthur as an enlightened thinker, someone who questions unfettered capitalist growth.

In addition, these chapters once again break the fourth wall, inserting omniscient narration to disrupt the plot. This creates situations of dramatic irony in which the reader is privy to a greater understanding of events and ideas than the characters themselves. Chapter 23, in its entirety, is a narrative intrusion, explaining the "important and popular fact that things are not always what they seem" (105). The chapter reveals that dolphins are more intelligent than humans, and that there is still yet another species more intelligent than humans besides the dolphins. This tantalizing hint is dropped before the characters become aware of said species' intelligence. The species "spent a lot of their time in behavioral research laboratories running round inside wheels and conducting frighteningly elegant and subtle experiments on man" (105). This information, paired with the earlier hint about Trillian's lost mice and the attention that should have been paid to their escape in Chapter 19, points to mice as the most intelligent species of all.

Slartibartfast eventually reveals the truth to Arthur when he explains that Earth was originally made by the Magratheans and that it was actually a super-intelligent computer commissioned by the mice, who are highly-evolved pandimensional beings. Not only does this information disrupt everything Arthur has ever thought about his home planet, it also calls into question every metaphysical assumption about existence he has ever considered. If Earth is "'an organic computer'" (110) and mice have "'been experimenting on [him]'" (109), then the reasonable philosophical question about the purpose of existence must be reframed to an absurd degree.

Further, the story behind Earth's commissioned creation ruptures humanity's understanding of itself. In the unending quest for the ultimate answer to the greatest question of life, the universe, and everything, a race of hyper-intelligent beings engineer a computer that spits out a wholly unsatisfying answer: Forty-two. This leads to the question of *what is the question*, which in turn leads to the commissioning of the organic super-computer called Earth. The philosophers' seven-and-a-half-million-year debate over what that deeply significant answer might be gives Adams the opportunity to satirize academia and the authority of "experts." As Deep Thought tells them, "'Everyone's going to have their own theories about what answer I'm eventually going to come up with, and who better to capitalize on that media market than you yourselves?'" (115).

Instead of portraying the philosophers as enlightened thinkers engaged with the most important questions of human existence, the author depicts them as closeted capitalists desiring fame and money. They are all given nonsensical names, like "Majikthise" and "Vroomfondel" (114). Their names are as ridiculous as their endless, fruitless pursuits, the author implies. The philosopher Phouchg's shallow pronouncement about Deep Thought's amazing creation that it calls Earth—"'What a dull name,'" he complains (122)—further underscores the philosophers' imaginative and intellectual impoverishment.

Chapters 29-35

Chapter 29 Summary

Trillian and Ford wake Zaphod up; the effects of the gas have mostly worn off. The three are standing in the middle of a simulated catalog of what Magrathea has to offer. Zaphod is particularly excited about the planet made of solid gold.

Soon the conversation returns to Zaphod's severing of certain parts of his own brain. He recalls some of his youthful exploits with a particular impresario, Yooden Vranx. Apparently it was Yooden who told him about the Heart of Gold and it was Yooden's idea that Zaphod should steal it. Thus, his bid for the presidency was a ruse, the only way in which he could access the unveiling in order to steal the ship with its Infinite Improbability Drive. The problem remains: He still does not know for what reason he wanted to steal the ship. Slartibartfast appears and informs the three that "'[t]he mice will see you now'" (126).

Chapter 30 Summary

Slartibartfast fills in the gaps for Zaphod, Trillian, and Ford about the original purpose of the custom-designed planet Earth. Arthur adds, "not unbitterly," that the planet was destroyed approximately five minutes before the calculations were complete (127). Slartibartfast, too, is upset; his fjord designs of Norway, for which he once won an award, are now gone. He is slated to work on Africa this time around, about which he is not very enthusiastic—no fjords to work on. Still, he soldiers on, informing the four that they are to meet the mice shortly, an event he claims is third in line as the most improbable in history.

Chapter 31 Summary

The chapter begins with a tangent about how "careless talk costs lives" (129). Arthur's joke at the end of the previous chapter has apparently caused a wormhole to open up, wherein his words carry to a world in which a battle is about to rage. His overheard words are considered an insult to one side, so the battle commences with great ferocity over thousands of years. When the species finally learns that the words came from the mouth of an Earthling, they spend several thousand years more tracking down the source on Earth, "where due to a terrible miscalculation of scale the entire battle fleet was accidentally swallowed by a small dog" (129).

The mice, called Benjy mouse and Frankie mouse, welcome the group to lunch. They announce that they will no longer need the rebuilt planet Earth; after all, they have an Earthman who was present during the last few moments of its existence. Besides, they are tired of the whole philosophical endeavor at this point, having invested millions of years in finding the answer to life, the universe, and everything only to have to invest several millions more in discovering the question. Now, they will only need Arthur's brain in order to extract the last bits of data. They are willing to pay for it and to replace it with a perfectly adequate electronic model: as Frankie puts it, "'a simple one will suffice'" (133). Arthur, however, is not willing to sell his brain and a chase ensues. Arthur and the others are cornered as men with grisly-looking medical equipment close in on them. The scene is interrupted by an ear-splitting alarm.

Chapter 32 Summary

The transportation devices the mice were using lies smashed on the floor, while their henchmen have all been knocked unconscious. Arthur and his companions have escaped. The mice debate what they should do now. They decide to "'try and fake a question'" and eventually settle on "'How many roads must a man walk down?'" (135). The answer to this could plausibly be "42." They figure they can make a killing on the lecture circuit.

Now, Arthur and cohort are being chased by cops who are after Zaphod for stealing the Heart of Gold. The cops appear rather disillusioned with their work, however, and a conversation ensues about how they would rather be doing other, more enjoyable activities. This distracts everyone for a moment before the cops start shooting at the group again.

Chapter 33 Summary

Suddenly, everything grows quiet. The cops have stopped shooting and everyone wonders whether the silence is a trap. Finally, Ford ventures out to check on the cops. They are all dead, as their life support systems all mysteriously failed. The group decides to escape using the aircar that

Arthur recognizes as Slartibartfast's vehicle. There is a simple note with an instruction on how to pilot the aircar: "This is probably the best button to press" (140).

Chapter 34 Summary

Ford is still pondering the mysterious nature of their escape as they run back to the ship. Meanwhile, the others "hurried back onto the Heart of Gold suffering from an acute attack of no curiosity" (141). They are surprised to see Marvin—"lying face down in the cold dust" (142)— waiting for them. He explains how much everyone hates him. Even the policecraft he tried to talk to despises him. When Ford asks what happened in the exchange, Marvin replies, "'It committed suicide'" (142) rather than continuing the conversation.

Chapter 35 Summary

The Heart of Gold is on its way again while Zaphod downs a Pan Galactic Gargle Blaster and Trillian and Ford are deep in thoughtful conversation. Arthur decides to take *The Hitchhiker's Guide to the Galaxy* to bed with him, noting that if he is going to have to live in the Universe, he might as well know as much as he can about it. He reads an entry that mentions lunch just as Zaphod buzzes him via the intercom to ask if he is hungry. Arthur replies that, yes, after all of these adventures, he is a bit hungry. So Zaphod turns the ship toward the Restaurant at the End of the Universe.

Chapters 29-35 Analysis

The last few chapters, like the book as a whole, are stacked with improbable events and timely coincidences. The randomness of the Universe—exacerbated in part by the Infinite Improbability Drive—seems to grow with each passing moment. The fact that the last surviving Earthman in the galaxy has arrived on the mythical planet Magrathea just as the mice are recommissioning the building of Earth II is another astronomical convergence of events. As Slartibartfast claims, this is "the third most improbable event in the history of the Universe" (128). When Arthur asks what the first two events were, Slartibartfast replies, "'Oh, probably just coincidences'" (128). Thus, yet again, the author conflates coincidence with providence. Adams ensures that the answers to such metaphysical conundrums—like the answer to the question of life, the universe, and everything—remain random, indecipherable, or at least nonsensical, furthering the theme of **Meaning VS Meaninglessness in Existence.**

The tangential aside that the narrator recounts at length in Chapter 31— about Arthur's words slipping through a wormhole and causing a thousand-year war—is yet another example of Adams's use of humor to create philosophical puzzles. As the narrator acknowledges of this random incident, "It is of course well known that careless talk costs lives, but the full scale of the problem is not always appreciated" (129). From the World War II slogan, "loose lips sink ships," to an interspatial wormhole in which a casually-uttered sentence unleashes full-scale warfare and destruction, Adams wields the "butterfly effect" to exaggerated ends. The "butterfly effect" derives from the field of chaos theory, suggesting that even the flap of a butterfly's wings can, given certain conditions of time and space, create a tornado several days later in another region of the globe. While Adams clearly satirizes such ideas, he also takes them seriously enough to demonstrate what happens when such ideas are taken to the furthest extremes of their implications. He questions scientific authority and knowledge in the same way in which he questions capitalist systems and governing bodies.

Another form of authority is questioned during the final scramble to escape. The cops' behavior and conversation while chasing the group satirizes the authority of law enforcement. When the cops defend their actions by suggesting that they would really rather not be yelling and shooting at other people, they also add that it is just a part of the job: "'Because there are some things you have to do even if you are an enlightened liberal cop who knows all about sensitivity and everything!'" one of them argues (137). Thus, the stereotypical banter an audience encounters in the average police drama turns into a satirical critique of the cops' actual duties. The satire works on two levels, both as a response to the cliches involved in the writing of cop shows and as an examination of the job of police officer itself.

The random nature of the cops' deaths also highlights the continuing flirtation with coincidence: It appears that Marvin's conversation with the police officers' vehicle ultimately led to their demise. His particular brand of passive-aggressive, depressive conversation incites the policecraft to commit death by suicide, as Marvin tells the group, which had the effect of cutting off the cops' life support systems. Arthur and his companions are therefore saved by a series of random events. First, the sounding of the alarm which interrupts the mice's plot to take Arthur's brain is initiated by the arrival of the cops who are searching for Zaphod

Beeblebrox. Second, Slartibartfast has randomly left them his aircar as a means of escape, presumably because he is disgruntled about the cancellation of the Earth II project—also initiated by the randomness of Arthur, the last Earthman, showing up coincidentally on Magrathea. Third, Marvin's casual conversation with another machine ultimately takes care of the cops who are chasing the group.

In the final moments of the book, the characters turn their attention towards eating lunch. Adams inflates the importance of an ordinary occasion, lunch, to exponential degrees. Arthur reads in *The Guide* that, "'[t]he history of every major Galactic Civilization tends to pass through three distinct and recognizable phases, those of Survival, Inquiry and Sophistication, otherwise known as How, Why and Where phases'" (143). This at first appears as if it were an academic discussion about the evolution of civilizations, but then *The Guide* turns to more mundane concerns in its example of these phases: "'For instance, the first phase is characterized by the question 'How can we eat?' the second by the question 'Why do we eat?' and the third by the question 'Where shall we have lunch?''" (143). Thus, the quotidian is conflated with the philosophical, the ordinariness of life mixed up with the great metaphysical questions of the universe—just like Arthur's ordinary house represents all of Earth and the threat to its continuing existence. There is meaning in life, the universe, and everything if one knows where to look —even if one does not know the question.

Character Analysis

Arthur Dent

Arthur Dent is an anti-hero Englishman who manages to save himself—and his companions—through sheer dumb luck. He has an awkward knack for speaking uncomfortable truths, as well as a naïve talent for stumbling into strange situations. Why Ford Prefect, his friend from Betelgeuse, chooses to rescue Arthur from the destruction of Earth remains a mystery, though Arthur's harmless charm and ironic good humor are quite disarming. Besides, it could simply be his destiny to accompany Ford on his exploits throughout the galaxy—or it could be mere coincidence. The author, with deliberate intention, does not make this distinction clear.

Arthur is initially described as a rather anxious, if ordinary, young man: "He was about thirty [. . .], tall, dark-haired and never quite at ease with himself. The thing that used to worry him was the fact that people always used to ask him what he was looking so worried about" (7). He appears to be content with his life, living in an unremarkable house outside London, but his life is upended when his house is slated to be demolished to make way for a bypass. It is further thrown into chaos by the inconvenient coincidence that Earth itself is slated to be demolished to make way for an interstellar highway. His rescue turns out to be a decidedly mixed bag: on the one hand, he is alive and experiencing adventures no Earthman has ever known. On the other hand, he is stuck traveling with a rogue band of rather shady characters who seem to find trouble wherever they go—not to mention the fact that the Earth itself, along with everything Arthur finds familiar and comforting, is gone.

As the central protagonist of the book, Arthur provides perspective for the reader, who is also thrown into this unfamiliar intergalactic (and absurd) world. When he thinks of Earth, he is saddened by its loss: "England only existed in his mind—his mind, stuck here in this dank smelly steel-lined spaceship" (43). Instead of considering his amazing luck, or waxing enthusiastic about the opportunities before him, Arthur broods over missing England. Later, he tries to convince the android Marvin that Earth was not "'awful,'" as the robot insists: "'Ah no, it was a beautiful place'" (100). This nostalgia for the Earth-that-was surely represents the author's fears for the planet and for human society, for the consumer capitalism that runs roughshod over nature and the static bureaucracies that impede on individual good will.

While Arthur remains relatively naïve up until the end—wincing at the mice on the dinner table, befuddled by his role in the unfolding drama—he also remains central to the group's survival, even if he is unconvinced of his own importance. However, it is his brain that might contain the clue that will reveal the question behind the puzzling answer to life, the universe, and everything. In spite of this, Arthur will not relinquish his brain, suggesting that Arthur is determined to hold on to what makes him unique and human, even at the cost of continued philosophical ignorance. At the novel's end, he is determined to make the best of an absurd situation. He picks up *The Hitchhiker's Guide to the Galaxy* and begins to read: "Since he was going to have to live in the place, [Arthur] reasoned, he'd better start finding out something about it" (143).

Ford Prefect

A foil to Arthur Dent's innocent character, Ford Prefect is an altogether different kind of anti-hero: he is a wordly traveler, a researcher for the irreverent guidebook, *The Hitchhiker's Guide to the Galaxy*, stuck on Earth for the past fifteen years. He is considered eccentric, with a prodigious talent for imbibing alcohol and regaling listeners with outlandish tales: "He struck most of the friends he had made on Earth as an eccentric, but a harmless one—an unruly boozer with some oddish habits" (11). He blended into his new surroundings fairly well, claiming to be an out-of-work actor for the past decade and a half—something his Earth friends found perfectly plausible. However, "[h]e had made one careless blunder," deciding on "the name 'Ford Prefect' as being nicely inconspicuous" (11). The Ford Prefect was a rather popular compact car produced in England by the Ford Motor Company between 1938 and 1961. Still, Ford manages to overcome this mistake because he "was not conspicuously tall, his features were striking but not conspicuously handsome" (11). His heroism derives from the sole fact that he is an alien with alien technology that serves to detect alien ships which can help him get off the planet before it is destroyed, dragging Arthur along with him.

Ford is conspicuous in one specific way: He is a rather cool character, both in the sense of keeping calm in the face of extraordinary circumstances and in the sense of being fashionable. For example, he always travels with his towel, which renders him ultra-cool. As *The Guide* notes, "What the strag [nonhitchhiker] will think is that any man who can hitch the length and breadth of the Galaxy, rough it, slum it, struggle against terrible odds, win through and still know where his towel is, is clearly a man to be reckoned with" (21). As *The Guide* renders it, in intergalactic slang, Ford is "a frood who really knows where his towel is," wherein "frood" describes a "really amazingly together guy" (21). A man of action, Ford always knows just what to do, even in the face of the infamously inhospitable Vogons. After all, "[h]e knew where his towel was" (25).

Zaphod Beeblebrox

The newly-elected President of the Galaxy, Zaphod Beeblebrox, is either an inspired con man or a frustrated genius, depending on the day and who one asks. On his securing of the presidency, the response is bemused: "Many had seen it as clinching proof that the whole of known creation had finally gone bananas" (27). What many do not know is that the President of the Galaxy has no power other than the power of disruption, the task of taking attention away from the actual centers of power. In this way, "Zaphod was amazingly good at his job" (29).

He arrives on the scene of the unveiling of the Heart of Gold, a gleaming new spaceship equipped with the Infinite Improbability Drive, in a speedboat, sending up arcs of water and churning the sea into great waves and plumes of foam. As the narrator explains, "Zaphod loved effect: it was what he was best at" (29). He is initially described as an "adventurer, ex-hippie, good-timer (crook? quite possibly), [and] manic self-publicist" (28). He also, quite uniquely, boasts two heads and a third arm, courtesy of elective personal enhancements. Thus, Zaphod is both a larger-than-life figure, purposefully cultivating an outsized image, and a familiar archetype—that of the charismatic outlaw who harbors a good heart underneath his rough-hewn exterior and questionable motives.

Zaphod is openly vain, obsessively tuning the radio for news of his exploits even as staggering coincidences—like the ship rescuing Arthur and Ford from outer space—pile up around him. He admits to Trillian that he would rather have saved the stowaways than leave them to die even though he is irritated by their presence. He portrays himself as an unflappable rogue, though underneath the showmanship, he is troubled by his lack of self-awareness. Later, the reader discovers that Zaphod has severed parts of his own brains in order to conceal his memories and motivations. He admits, in a moment of uncharacteristic honesty, that "'whenever I stop and think—why did I want to do something?—how did I work out how to do it?—I get a very strong desire just to stop thinking about it. Like I have now. It's a big effort to talk about it'" (97). In this way, Zaphod becomes a metaphor for modern alienation: He is a stranger to himself.

Trillian (a.k.a. Patricia MacMillan)

While Trillian is a minor character in the book, she is significant because of her connection to Earth and to Arthur, albeit tenuously. Her presence embodies the astronomical improbabilities that have brought the cast of characters together. She is first introduced as "a girl that Zaphod had picked up recently while visiting a planet, just for fun, incognito" (31), which minimizes both her importance and her agency. In fact, Trillian is incredibly intelligent, highly-educated, and more than a little adventurous. Explaining her decision to hitch a ride with Zaphod, she remarks, "'After all, with a degree in math and another in astrophysics what else was there to do? It was either that or the dole queue again on Monday'" (74). This is both an acknowledgment of Trillian's superior intellect and a satirical assessment of the employability of academics— an acerbic comment on British society as well as the academy itself.

Trillian is also an intertwined part of the improbable set of coincidences that manifest throughout the book. She is not only from Earth, she also knows Arthur, having met him at a party before ditching him in favor of Zaphod. It turns out that the number representing the improbability of Arthur and Ford's rescue from deep space, in "a totally staggering coincidence" (54), happens to be the telephone number to the apartment on Earth where Trillian met both Arthur and Zaphod. Later, the book implies that the telephone number is, in fact, Trillian's number (70).

Trillian also brings the mice aboard the ship, who turn out to be extraordinarily significant to the plot. In addition, she is perceptive, seeing through Zaphod's bravado by recognizing "he never really understood the significance of anything he did" (62) and becoming weary of his showy antics. Her calm intellect serves as the antithesis to Zaphod's sometimes false and always exaggerated bravado.

Marvin the Depressed Android

Marvin the robot embodies existential dread. The onboard android for the Heart of Gold, Marvin has been programmed with a Genuine People Personality, albeit one that is thoroughly unpleasant. Marvin's posture projects abject despair, with his head hanging between his knees and his voice "low and hopeless" (64) while his body shakes with "spasm[s] of despair" when asked to perform any duty (65). He bemoans his job and his very existence. He is christened "'the Paranoid Android'" by Zaphod, while Arthur dubs him an "'electronic sulking machine'" (103).

Ironically enough, however, Marvin—who hates humans, as the narrator reminds the reader several times—saves the group's lives. The act is decidedly unintentional, though, and Marvin uses the incident to bolster his self-pity. When the humans are nearly captured by the intergalactic police who are hunting Zaphod, Marvin strikes up a conversation with their policecraft, a vehicle responsible for maintaining the cops' life support systems. Marvin tells the humans, "'I talked to the computer at great length and explained my view of the Universe to it'" (142), which incites the overburdened computer to die by suicide, cutting off life support to the cops. Thus, the humans are able to escape unscathed in spite of Marvin's misanthropic tendencies.

Themes

The Absurdity of Modern Bureaucracy

From Arthur's run-in with the local council and planning office to the incompetent intergalactic civil servants, unchecked bureaucracy runs rampant throughout *The Hitchhiker's Guide to the Galaxy*. Not only does Arthur Dent lose his personal home, he also loses his planetary one, both casualties of the faceless bureaucratic entities that exercise their power without empathy. Adams suggests that the Galaxy is no different than the Earth: bureaucratic ineptitude, thoughtless development schemes, and job dissatisfaction mark the modern age.

Arthur's confrontation with bureaucracy comes as his house is scheduled to be demolished to make way for a new bypass. When Arthur questions Mr. L. Prosser about the purpose of the bypass, Prosser provides a wholly unsatisfactory answer, an example of circular reasoning: "'What do you mean, why's it got to be built? [. . .] It's a bypass. You've got to build bypasses'" (9). Prosser's answer reveals the truth at the heart of bureaucratic fiats: The entire enterprise exists to justify itself. Prosser represents the quintessential bureaucrat as he would rather be anywhere than there, dealing with another disgruntled citizen: "He shifted his weight from foot to foot [. . .] Obviously somebody had been appallingly incompetent and he hoped to God it wasn't him" (9). Prosser is not so much interested in resolving the dispute with Arthur as he is in placing the blame somewhere else. Bureaucratic hierarchies facilitate evasion of personal responsibility, making it virtually impossible for Arthur to question or resist what is happening.

The Vogons also represent the same bureaucratic workings in their demolition of the Earth to make way for a hyperspatial bypass. Like Prosser, Prostetnic Vogon Jeltz does not really relish his job; he does it because it has to be done: "He always felt vaguely irritable after demolishing populated planets. He wished that someone would come and tell him that it was all wrong so that he could shout at them and feel better" (36). Again, the reasoning is circular, the job is self-justifying. In addition, the Earth could have been saved had a report reached Prostetnic Vogon Jeltz in time, as "a wonderful new form of spaceship drive [. . .] would henceforth make all hyperspatial express routes unnecessary" (36). The news exposes the pointlessness and inefficiency of destroying Earth, suggesting that it is the nature of bureaucracy to never consider the consequences of its actions—or, even, the relevance of its purpose. As Slartibartfast puts it, when the entire story of Earth is recounted—ten million years of evolutionary history wiped out in the work of a moment—"'Well, that's bureaucracy for you'" (127).

Even the legendary Magrathea is not above the gravitational pull of bureaucracy. Its automated messages to the approaching Heart of Gold—not to mention its oncoming missiles—are generated by an ancient, and defunct, governing body. The messages themselves are redolent with the language of officialdom: "The commercial council of Magrathea thanks you for your esteemed visit [. . .] but regrets [. . .] that the entire plant is temporarily closed for business'" (84). First, this automated voice lies: The inhabitants are merely in hypersleep, not away and unable to do business. Second, it masks its threatening intentions with an officious tone, laced with bureaucratic jargon, calling its missiles "part of a special service we extend to all of our most enthusiastic clients" (84). The absurdity of the situation becomes clear in the juxtaposition between the courteous language and the deadly intention. Once again, bureaucracy operates in illogical and pointlessly destructive ways.

There is another unintended consequence of the byzantine bureaucratic systems that populate the book: extreme job dissatisfaction, itself another byproduct of the capitalist imperatives of the modern age. Mr. L. Prosser clearly does not enjoy his job, just as the Vogon captain also despises his work. When asked why he does his job, the young Vogon assigned to take Arthur and Ford Prefect to the airlock has no ready answer: "'I dunno. I think I just sort of . . . do it really. My aunt said that spaceship guard was a good career for a young Vogon'" (49). Later, the Magrathean designer, Slartibartfast, reveals the pointlessness of his life's work: All those complicated, award-winning fjords he designed for the coast of Norway are simply vaporized in a flash of bureaucratic confusion. Finally, the cops sent to arrest Zaphod Beeblebrox for the theft of the Heart of Gold engage in a discussion about their own jobs, complaining, "'It isn't easy being a cop!'" (136) while insisting that they do not actually wish to shoot people. All of these examples reveal a deep disillusionment with work, an alienation from the functions demanded by a job made necessary by a consumer capitalist society. Bureaucracy, and the kind of work it engenders, generates many discontents of modernity.

The Emptiness of Authority

Throughout the novel, different kinds of authority—governmental, institutional, academic—are exposed as empty or corrupt. From Zaphod Beeblebrox's comic ascent to the presidency to the institutional authority of the academy to the challenges of authorship, the book skewers any claims to authority. Authority possesses no legitimate reason for being; it exists only insofar as it legitimizes itself, much like bureaucracy. In this sense, authority is akin to authoring fiction: one can simply make it up as one goes along.

In explaining Zaphod Beeblebrox's new position as President of the Imperial Galactic Government, the narrator reveals that this alleged position of authority has no literal power at all, calling the President "very much a figurehead" with "no real power whatsoever" (28). The President is all style and no substance, meant to serve as a distraction from the real wielding of power that takes place out of the public eye: "His job is not to wield power but to draw attention away from it" (28). Zaphod Beeblebrox is essentially a confidence man who flaunts his eccentricities and attracts the public's attention with his antics. The narrator also skewers the inflated claim to authority embedded in the continued use of the term "Imperial" in the title, calling it "an anachronism" and describing how the last "hereditary Emperor" was "locked in a stasis field which keeps him in a state of perpetual unchangingness" at the time of his death (28). The dead Emperor's state of "perpetual unchangingness" can be read as a specific critique of the British monarchy—an anachronistic institution forever frozen in time—and as a general critique of the ways in which authority self-referentially reinforces itself. It is not enough for the title to be "President" of the Galaxy, it must also suggest something grander and more persuasive—the "*Imperial* Galactic Government."

Academic authority is also satirized. The institutional staidness of the *Encyclopedia Galactica* is no match for the colorful anarchy of *The Hitchhiker's Guide to the Galaxy*, which "sells rather better" than the stodgy reference book (17). Another example involves the invention of the Infinite Improbability Drive. It is not invented by an established expert, but by a student sweeping up in the lab: "He [. . .] was rather startled to discover that he had managed to create the long-sought-after golden Infinite Improbability generator out of thin air" (60). The ruckus that ensues also lampoons academics: Upon receiving an award for his work, the student is "lynched by a rampaging mob of respectable physicists who had finally realized that the one thing they really couldn't stand was a smart-ass" (60). The event undermines the authority of the establishment by presenting a mere student as the author of scientific progress, while also exposing the self-serving pettiness and jealousy of the seemingly "respectable" scientists themselves.

Adams also questions the authority inherent to authorship, as exemplified in his frequent breaking of the "fourth wall." In so doing, the author implicitly acknowledges both his omniscience and his artifice: The novel is a work of fiction, created by an all-knowing author—who is all-knowing only because he creates the fictional world—wherein the characters are manipulated in order to meet the author's ends. This is an inclusionary form of authority, as the author's assertion of omniscience is only made possible by his admission of artificiality—*anybody* can make things up. Ultimately, this may be the only kind of authority for which Adams can advocate: the kind that admits its claim to sovereignty comes from openly fictionalizing characters and events.

Meaning VS Meaninglessness in Existence

At the heart of the book is a struggle over coming to terms with the meaning—or potential meaninglessness—of existence. Adams often conflates coincidence with destiny and vice versa, never quite confirming which might dictate the rules of his fictional world. In addition, metaphysical musings over life, the universe, and everything are simultaneously satirized and taken seriously. Ultimately, there are fewer answers than there are questions, and the answers are often unsatisfying or absurd.

When Arthur and Ford are picked up by the Heart of Gold, the astronomical odds against them are mentioned more than once, with "the chances of getting picked up by another ship" presented as virtually impossible due to the "mind-boggling size" of space (53-54). Nevertheless, Arthur and Ford are rescued by mere coincidence, the randomness unleashed by the Infinite Improbability Drive, or possibly because they have necessary roles to play in the unfolding narrative. Destiny implies purpose while coincidence is mere happenstance, yet it is never entirely clear which force is at play. In another moment of barely-believable coincidence—or, conversely, destiny—Arthur asserts that he has actually met Zaphod Beeblebrox before. While Ford struggles to grasp this incredibly unlikely connection, Trillian comes onto the bridge. She is the reason that Arthur and Zaphod have met; they were both vying for her attention at a party back on Earth some months ago. The improbability of the convergence of these particular characters grows more inconceivable with each passing scene, leaving open the question as to whether such events are all random or destiny-driven.

The metaphysical musings on the nature of existence also grapple with the problem of purpose and are often entangled with the absurdity of improbability and coincidence. When the Infinite Improbability Drive diverts the Heart of Gold from the path of missiles, the missiles themselves transform into a sperm whale and a bowl of petunias. Both apparitions contemplate the meaning of existence. In the first case, the whale "had very little time to come to terms with its identity" before hitting the planet's surface, but still manages to ask the central questions: "[W]ho am I? [. . .] Why am I here? What's my purpose in life?" (90). The implication is that all sentient creatures are primed to interrogate such metaphysical conundrums. In the second case, the bowl of petunias thinks, "Oh no, not again" (91). As the narrator continues, "Many people have speculated that if we knew exactly why the bowl of petunias had thought that we would know a lot more about the nature of the Universe than we do now" (91). Adams's Universe is not merely random—the bowl of petunias *has been here before*—but peppered with hints about the potential interconnectedness of people, events, and the Universe itself.

The ultimately elusive purpose of existence is why philosophers are satirized so extensively in the novel, with Adams ridiculing their confidence in finding definitive answers. When Deep Thought is reactivated after millions of years to reveal his answer, one of the philosopher pundits expresses total confidence in the computer's response: "'Never again [. . .] will we wake up in the morning and think *Who am I? What is my purpose in life?*" (118). However, the philosopher's over-confident enthusiasm is immediately undermined by Deep Thought's confusing answer: The answer to life, the universe, and everything is Forty-two. The great computer goes on to suggest that the philosophers do not even understand the question they were asking. The implication is that to answer such a question is to undermine the actual purpose of life—which is to continue asking such questions as "*What is my purpose in life?*" If humanity found definitive answers, Adams suggests, the very essence of what makes them human would be lost.

Symbols & Motifs

The Insignificance of Earth

The motif of Earth's ultimate insignificance is launched at the novel's opening, with a description of Earth's place within the larger Galaxy. It exists "Far out in the uncharted backwaters of the unfashionable end" of the Galaxy, where "a small unregarded yellow sun" provides the heat and light necessary for life on "an utterly insignificant little blue-green planet" (5) that is the Earth. Earth is inconsequential, unimportant—even *unfashionable*—to the Galaxy as a whole. Furthermore, Earth's people are unhappy, obsessed with money and consumerism, and not very sophisticated in general. When a woman has a revelation about how to help the people of Earth attain happiness, the Earth is shortly destroyed thereafter. Thus, "nearly two thousand years after one man [the Biblical Jesus] had been nailed to a tree for saying how great it would be to be nice to people for a change" (5), the messenger is again annihilated. The Earth is destroyed in order to make way for an hyperspatial bypass— which, it turns out, has been rendered obsolete by new technology and will never be built anyway.

Therefore, contrary to what its inhabitants may believe, Earth is most certainly not the center of the known Universe. However, the Earth is simultaneously more and less important than initially expected. It is a kind of biological computer, designed by a hyperintelligent race, to determine the question to the answer of life, the universe, and everything. In this respect, the Earth is quite significant, as it is central to the quest for the ultimate answer to the puzzle of existence, yet even this significance is satirized and undermined: The hyperintelligent race is made up of mice, who are a superior lifeform to humans. When Deep Thought names the computer-planet "Earth," the hyperintelligent philosophers are unimpressed: "'What a dull name,'" one pronounces (122). Thus, the ultimate insignificance of Earth is still reinserted, with Adams parodying the assumption that the Earth—along with its unsophisticated inhabitants—is central to the Universe.

The Hitchhiker's Guide to the Galaxy e-book

The Guide within *The Hitchhiker's Guide to the Galaxy* becomes a symbol of accessible knowledge and discovery in the novel while also functioning as a meta-fictive element. *The Guide* is an electronic book filled with entries on the galaxy and is a best-selling phenomenon. *The Guide* "has already supplanted the great *Encyclopedia Galactica* as the standard repository of all knowledge and wisdom" (6), with *The Guide's* runaway success the result of two specific differences: "First, it is slightly cheaper; and second, it has the words DON'T PANIC inscribed in large friendly letters on its cover" (6). Arthur consults the *Guide* throughout the novel, with the *Guide* providing explanations and advice about the Universe Arthur is now navigating. In a Universe filled with uncertainty and danger, the *Guide* provides a reassuring presence, and is the only source of authority not entirely mocked or undermined in the narrative, suggesting that literature can still be a source of enlightenment and entertainment. In creating an actual *Guide* within his own book, Adams suggests, in a meta-fictional fashion, that his own book is both a repository of vast knowledge and great wisdom.

The Babel Fish

The Babel fish is a potent symbol in the debate over whether there exists an intelligent higher power. Its name is an allusion to the Biblical story of the Tower of Babel, in which mankind angers God by attempting to build a tower together that can reach heaven. In response to mankind's attempts, God creates multiple languages and scatters humans all over the earth, to make such united attempts at challenging his powers more difficult in future. The Babel fish in the novel is therefore an ironic answer to the problem of universal communication, as it once more provides a means by which humans can understand one another effortlessly. The "small yellow fish" appears unassuming, but allows for any language to be immediately comprehensible to the listener when placed within the ear. The controversy over such an unlikely and highly useful creature has reverberated throughout the Universe, with "such a bizarrely improbably coincidence that anything so mind-bogglingly useful could have evolved purely by chance" causing quite a metaphysical stir (42).

Many suggest that the Babel fish proves the existence of God. However, others suggest that the Babel fish presents "'final and clinching proof of the *non*existence of God'" (42). The debate leads to a best-selling book by Oolon Colluphid, entitled *Well That About Wraps It Up for God.* Adams utilizes the symbolism of the Babel fish to raise questions about the metaphysical possibilities for an intelligent higher power, or God, while also raising the age-old issue of cross-cultural and crosslinguistic communication. As with every metaphysical conundrum introduced within the book, there is no concrete answer. The narrator ends the discussion on the Babel fish by noting, via *The Guide*, that it "'has caused more and bloodier wars than anything else in the history of creation'" (42), turning a tool for potential unity into, once again, a source of disunity and conflict.

The Number 42

While the Number 42 appears only briefly in the novel as the answer to life, the universe, and everything, it becomes a notable symbol of Adams's satirical take on the wider philosophical search for meaning. The Earth is commissioned by the mice as a super-computer in order to calculate the question, only for the Earth to be destroyed a few minutes before it has finished its many millions of years of calculations. Thus, after Arthur—the only surviving Earthling—escapes from the mice with his brain intact, the mice have no other option than to invent a question. These events reveal the fundamental absurdity of seeking a *conclusive* answer to the existential questions of the *ultimate* meaning of life: Adams is not merely satirizing the infinitely improbable search for such a definitive answer but also slyly suggesting that, if humanity ever *did* actually come up with an answer, it would be profoundly disappointing.

Important Quotes

1. "Bypasses are devices that allow some people to dash from Point A to Point B very fast while other people dash from Point B to Point A very fast. People living at Point C, being a point directly in between, are often given to wonder what's so great about Point A that so many people from Point B are so keen to get there, and what's so great about Point B that so many people from Point A are so keen to get there. They often wish that people would just once and for all work out where the hell they wanted to be."
(Chapter 1, Page 9)

An example of Adams's satirical humor, this passage pokes fun at the frantic pace and restlessness of modern life. Everyone rushes around constantly, wanting (or needing) to get from one place to another as quickly as possible, with nobody ever fully at ease with where they are. In addition, the passage implicitly critiques the demands of a society obsessed with capitalist consumption and the work necessary to afford the material goods one thinks one needs.

2. "'Drink up,' said Ford, 'you've got three pints to get through.'
'Three pints? said Arthur. 'At lunchtime?'
The man sitting next to Ford grinned and nodded happily. Ford ignored him. He said, 'Time is an illusion. Lunchtime doubly so.'"
(Chapter 2, Page 18)

This passage makes a humorous aside of the important metaphysical and astrophysical conundrums of the age. The idea that time itself may not be as concretely real as humans experience it is fundamental to an understanding of Einstein's Special Theory of Relativity, or quantum physics. The idea that lunchtime is even more elusive adds to the irreverent humor of the passage.

3. "The contents of Ford Prefect's satchel were quite interesting [. . .] Besides the Sub-Etha Sens-O-Matic and the scripts he had an Electronic Thumb—a short black rod, smooth and matt with a couple of flat switches and dials at one end; he also had a device that looked rather

like a largish electronic calculator. [. . .] Beneath that in Ford Prefect's satchel were a few ballpoints, a notepad and a largish bath towel from Marks and Spencer."
(Chapter 3, Pages 20 - 21)

Ford is equipped with all of the items crucial to his work not only as an intrepid researcher for The Hitchhiker's Guide to the Galaxy *but also to his travels as a hitchhiker. Adams's inventions here presage an age wherein GPS technology, cell phones, and e-books have become a part of the modern landscape. His nomenclature, in contrast, is derived directly from the names and marketing material of products from the post-World War II period. The "O-Matic" was a common suffix appended to what appeared to be futuristic products of the day (Veg-O-Matic, for example).*

4. "Beneath it [the dome] lay uncovered a huge spaceship, one hundred and fifty meters long, shaped like a sleek running show, perfectly white and mind-bogglingly beautiful. At the heart of it, unseen, lay a small gold box which carried within it the most brain-wrenching device ever conceived, a device that made this starship unique in the history of the Galaxy, a device after which the ship had been named—the Heart of Gold."
(Chapter 4, Page 32)

The Infinite Improbability Drive, that "brain-wrenching device," allows the Heart of Gold to travel infinite distances with improbable speed. Essentially, the device does not adhere to any logical scientific principles whatsoever—its very name elicits impossibility. However, it allows for Adams to explore the nature of coincidence, destiny, and the meaning of existence in both serious and absurd ways.

5. "The fact that [the Vogons survived] is some kind of tribute to the thick-willed slug-brained stubbornness of these creatures. *Evolution?* they said to themselves, *Who needs it?*, and what nature refused to do for them they simply did without until such time as they were able to rectify the gross anatomical inconveniences with surgery."
(Chapter 5, Page 33)

This description of the Vogons conjures up their essence as unevolved and unenlightened creatures for which the narrator, The Guide, and the characters have contempt. The fact that this galactic species also serves as the largest contingent in the Galactic Civil Service reinforces the author's satire of bureaucracy, with of the many bureaucratic servants being as unpleasant, unnecessary, and generally unbearable as the bureaucracies they serve.

6. "'Resistance is useless,' bellowed the guard, and then added, 'You see, if I keep it up I can eventually get promoted to Senior Shouting Officer, and there aren't usually many vacancies for nonshouting and nonpushing-people-about officers, so I think I'd better stick to what I know.'"
(Chapter 7, Page 50)

This is an example of the self-justifying nature of bureaucratic work —"Senior Shouting Officer" is a useless title in order to legitimize unnecessary work—as well as the intellectual and cultural constriction inherent to bureaucratic jobs. The young guard seeks out promotion for its own sake, rather than psychological or spiritual fulfillment—a clear critique of the capitalist impulse.

7. "The simple truth is that interstellar distances will not fit into the human imagination."
(Chapter 8, Page 53)

It is not that the human imagination is limited, but that "interstellar distances" are so large that they are simply beyond human comprehension. The passage appears as Arthur and Ford are launched out into space from the Vogon airlock. The passage underscores the astronomical improbability of their coincidental rescue by the passing Heart of Gold. Their rescue is so improbable that coincidence begins to look like destiny, although the narrative never offers a definitive answer as to whether fate exists.

8. "The Universe jumped, froze, quivered and splayed out in several unexpected directions."
(Chapter 9, Page 56)

This passage describes the widespread effect and power of the Infinite Improbability Drive, which can even turn nuclear missiles into a whale and a bowl of petunias. The Drive's power underscores both the improbable nature of the machine and the absurdist humor that can be wrung from such a trope, as it helps to both advance the novel's plot while creating improbable coincidences for the characters.

9. "'If there's anything more important than my ego around, I want it caught and shot now,' Zaphod glared at her again, then laughed."
(Chapter 12, Page 68)

The passage summarizes Zaphod's fundamental self-absorption while also satirizing the corruption of political power. As President, Zaphod should ideally be concerned with the general welfare of others, but instead, he only cares for his "ego" and wants anything that challenges his own importance to be "caught and shot," suggesting that Zaphod is always driven by self-serving ends in all of his antics.

10. "The Heart of Gold fled on silently through the night of space, now on conventional photon drive. Its crew of four were ill at ease knowing that they had been brought together not of their own volition or by simple coincidence, but by some curious perversion of physics—as if relationships between people were susceptible to the same laws that governed the relationships between atoms and molecules."
(Chapter 14, Page 75)

The passage once again conflates coincidence with destiny, social relationships with quantum physics. This passage foreshadows the revelation that the Earth is actually a kind of organic computer, wherein the mathematical algorithms presumably bring certain people together and make particular events occur. It is left unclear who, or what, is directing these events: artificial intelligence, divine intelligence, or sheer Universal randomness.

11. "'Can you fly her?' asked Ford pleasantly.
'No, can you?'
'No.'
'Trillian, can you?'
'No.'
'Fine,' said Zaphod, relaxing. We'll do it together.'
'I can't either,' said Arthur, who felt it was time he began to assert himself.'"
(Chapter 17, Page 86)

This exchange reveals important aspects of Arthur's characterization. He is ignored in the conversation about who can fly the ship, because his interstellar skills are non-existent. He is offended by the snub, though not vehemently, as he is aware of his short-comings. He does, however, start to "assert himself," suggesting growing self-confidence as he undergoes his space travels.

12. "Of all the planets in all the star systems of the Galaxy—many wild and exotic, seething with life—didn't he just have to turn up at a dump like this after fifteen years of being a castaway? Not even a hot-dog stand in evidence."
(Chapter 20, Page 94)

This passage is Ford's bleak assessment of Magrathea—or at least, the surface of Magrathea. It also provides a hint into Ford's character: He is eager to be engaged with the Universe again, after his long exile on Earth. His feelings of disappointment at discovering that the legendary planet is a "dump" that lacks even a "hot-dog stand" creates a moment of literary bathos, in which a character's sorrow is rendered in terms that elicit humor instead of pity.

13. "'I don't know what I'm looking for.'"
(Chapter 20, Page 97)

Zaphod's comment encapsulates the core metaphysical conundrum at the heart of the book, the existential riddle of the meaning of life. Zaphod also embodies the notion that sentient beings are alienated from themselves: He has severed his own minds, obscuring his motivations and memories even to himself. He seeks fame and fortune—to be President of the Galaxy, to steal the Heart of Gold, to find the fabulously wealthy Magrathea—and yet finds nothing satisfying. He is still looking for a greater truth or deeper meaning.

14. "When one day an expedition was sent to the spatial coordinates that Voojagig had claimed for this planet they discovered only a small asteroid inhabited by a solitary old man who claimed repeatedly that nothing was true, though he was later discovered to be lying."
(Chapter 21, Page 100)

In another tangential aside, Adams addresses the relativity of truth. In searching for the planet of sentient ballpoint pens, all that was found was "a solitary old man" engaged in espousing the relativity of the truth—that is, that "nothing was true." Ironically, however, the old man is lying.

15. "The last ever dolphin message was misinterpreted as a surprisingly sophisticated attempt to do a double-backward somersault through a

hoop while whistling the 'Star-Spangled Banner,' but in fact the message was this: *So long and thanks for all the fish.*"
(Chapter 23, Page 105)

As the narrator explains to the reader, the dolphins are the second most intelligent species on Earth, with humankind in third place. Here, the author parodies the human tendency to place themselves at the pinnacle of the planet's hierarchy: The dolphins are not performing mere tricks for the humans, they are trying to send them an important message. The dolphins know of the eminent destruction of Earth and cannot get the humans to understand, so they send a final message before their escape. This message becomes the title of the fourth book in the Hitchhiker *series.*

16. "Many millions of years ago a race of hyperintelligent pandimensional beings (whose manifestations in their own pandimensional universe is not dissimilar to our own) got so fed up with the constant bickering about the meaning of life which used to interrupt their favorite pastime of Brockian Ultra Cricket (a curious game which involved suddenly hitting people for no apparent reason and then running away) that they decided to sit down and solve their problems once and for all."
(Chapter 25, Page 111)

This passage is the background that Slartibartfast provides on the mice: They are the "hyperintelligent pandimensional beings" who commission the original computer, Deep Thought, to determine the answer to life, the universe, and everything. The mice's "constant bickering about the meaning of life" and their "curious game" of "suddenly hitting people for no apparent reason" parodies both mankind's own philosophical pretensions and propensity for meaningless violence.

17. "'You just let machines get on with the adding up,' warned Majikthise, 'and we'll take care of the eternal verities, thank you very much [. . .] Under the law the Quest for Ultimate Truth is quite clearly the inalienable prerogative of your working thinkers. Any bloody machine goes and actually *finds* it and we're straight out of a job, aren't we? I mean, what's the use of our sitting up half the night arguing that there may or may not be a God if this machine only goes and gives you his bleeding phone number the next morning?'"
(Chapter 25, Pages 114 - 115)

This passage satirizes bureaucratic and academic institutions. Majikthise is not actually interested in finding the answer to the meaning of life, as is his professional task—rather, he is more concerned with protecting his job security. The philosophers argue that Deep Throat will effectively render their profession obsolete. Majikthise's complaints that the computer will leave them "straight out of a job" once again reveals the self-serving and shallow motives of the novel's experts, who care more for their own social and intellectual standing than finding any definitive truths.

18. "'I speak of none but the computer that is to come after me,' intoned Deep Thought, his voice regaining its accustomed declamatory tones. 'A computer whose merest operational parameters I am not worthy to calculate—and yet I will design it for you. A computer that can calculate the Question to the Ultimate Answer, a computer of such infinite and subtle complexity that organic life shall itself form part of its operational matrix.'"
(Chapter 28, Page 122)

Deep Thought talks majestically about his design, ultimately to be called the Earth, which will incorporate "'organic life'" into its technological matrix. In having to create a new super-computer that will formulate the right question to the answer to life (Number 42), the passage parodies the endless—and ultimately futile—search for definitive meaning that humans (and the mice) are embarked upon.

19. "In the sky a huge sign appeared, replacing the catalog number. It said, *Whatever your tastes, Magrathea can cater for you. We are not proud.*"
(Chapter 29, Page 124)

This passage satirizes consumer capitalism, with the Magrathean advertisement parodying the relationship between producers and consumers. They will do anything—compromise their principles, bend the laws of physics, suspend moral judgement—in order to please their customers. Magrathea itself is the epitome of capitalist impulses run amok, as it bankrupts the Galaxy with its amassing of wealth.

20. "'In this replacement Earth we're rebuilding they've given me Africa to do and of course I'm doing it with all fjords again because I happen to like them, and I'm old-fashioned enough to think that they give a lovely baroque feel to a continent. And they tell it's not equatorial enough.

Equatorial!' He gave a hollow laugh. 'What does it matter? Science has achieved some wonderful things, of course, but I'd far rather be happy than right any day.'"
(Chapter 30, Page 128)

Slartibartfast's complaint about his new role in the rebuilding of Earth II echoes the many dissatisfied comments about work throughout the book. When work is divorced from beauty and pleasure, or spiritual and psychological fulfillment, then it is a drudgery. Slartibartfast represents the opposite of the young Vogon guard: He symbolizes the pursuit of artistic accomplishment over the bureaucratized roles imposed by institutions, wanting to be "happy" instead of "right" in his professional pursuits.

21. "'Well, I mean, *yes* idealism, *yes* the dignity of pure research, *yes* the pursuit of truth in all its forms, but there comes a point I'm afraid where you begin to suspect that if there's any *real* truth, it's that the entire multidimensional infinity of the Universe is almost certainly being run by a bunch of maniacs.'"
(Chapter 31, Pages 132 - 133)

In this passage, Frankie mouse replies to Arthur's query regarding the Ultimate Question. Arthur displays shock at the mice's willingness to fabricate a question, or at least to compromise ethically in collaborating on what makes best sense to the masses. The mice are interested in appearances rather than substance—the quest for truth and the adhering to ideals fall by the wayside in the pursuit of fame and fortune. Adams satirizes this self-serving impulse throughout the book, from the untitled introduction to the very end.

22. "'All right,' said Benjy. '*What do you get if you multiply six by seven?* 'No, no, too literal, too factual,' said Frankie, 'wouldn't sustain the punters' interest.'"
(Chapter 32, Page 135)

Proof of their cynical intentions, the mice collaborate in a ruse to invent a question that would cohere with the answer (forty-two) to life, the universe, and everything. The question, however, needs to be philosophically-engaging enough to prolong the never-ending debate about the meaning of existence and to please the "pundits." Keeping the people's interest is integral to the mice's desire to ensure lasting fame and fortune.

23. "'Let's get shot out of this whole,' said Zaphod. 'If whatever I'm supposed to be looking for is here, I don't want it.'"
(Chapter 33, Page 140)

While this statement is casually offered in the aftermath of a potentially deadly pursuit by police, Zaphod appears to be coming to terms with a fundamental truth. He keeps seeking fame and fortune—which Magrathea symbolizes—but this pursuit leaves him empty and endangered. He might be edging toward the realization that there is more to life than adventurous exploits engineered to keep him famous and wealthy.

24. "Ford could sense it and found it most mysterious—a ship and two policemen seemed to have gone spontaneously dead. In his experience the Universe simply didn't work like that."
(Chapter 34, Page 141)

This passage is ironic, since the Universe has been working at a highly improbable level throughout the entire novel. All of the coincidences the crew have experienced imply that the Universe is filled with implausible happenstance, while Ford's continued incredulity hints at a continuing reluctance to accept the randomness and unpredictability of existence.

25. "That night, as the Heart of Gold was busy putting a few lightyears between itself and the Horsehead Nebula, Zaphod lounged under the small palm tree on the bridge trying to bang his brain into shape with massive Pan Galactic Gargle Blasters; Ford and Trillian sat in a corner discussing life and matters arising from it; and Arthur took to his bed to flip through Ford's copy of *The Hitchhiker's Guide to the Galaxy*."
(Chapter 35, Page 143)

At the end of the novel, Zaphod ruminates, Ford and Trillian ponder the meaning of existence, and Arthur turns to the Guide *to better understand the Universe. Arthur's final scene with the* Guide *creates another meta-fictive moment in the novel, while once more suggesting that literature may be the one form of authority that remains authentic and valid.*

Essay Topics

1. How does the narrator characterize the Earth throughout the book? How is the Earth viewed by the main characters (Arthur, Ford, Zaphod, and Trillian)? What thematic and/or symbolic significance does Earth have in the novel?

2. Consider the role of bureaucracy and bureaucrats in the novel. How are they depicted? What is their wider significance?

2 questions answer both

3. Compare and contrast the various characters, who often work as foils for one another. How are Arthur and Ford similar or different? How does Zaphod's character compare and/or contrast to both Arthur and Ford? What role does Trillian or Marvin play in this dynamic?

3 questions answer all 3 compare and Contrast

4. From governments to academia to police agencies, the book tackles the complex question of how authority functions and how the individual is affected by systems of power. What forms of power exist in the novel? How is power used or misused? How do different characters respond to it?

3 questions

5. How does the author use science and technology to create his science-fictional world? How does Adams use his technological concepts to parody or illuminate aspects of his own era?

2 questions

6. *The Guide* within *The Hitchhiker's Guide to the Galaxy* represents another layer of narration. What is the effect of meta-fictional elements in the book? What does the *Guide* represent, and how does it function narratively and thematically?

3 questions

7. What is the impact of the Infinite Improbability Drive on the characters? On the plot? How does the author use this device to explore metaphysical conundrums?

3 questions

8. How does the author critique consumer capitalism? How does he portray work?

2 questions

9. Analyze the role of the mice and their society in the novel. What is their significance? Do they mirror humans and human society in any way? Why or why not?

4 questions

10. What does *The Hitchhiker's Guide to the Galaxy* suggest about the meaning of life, the universe, and everything?

3 questions

Made in the USA
Coppell, TX
01 July 2023

18669915R00036